EL SALVADOR

IS MY HOME

For a free color catalog describing Gareth Stevens' list of high-quality books, call 1-800-341-3569 (USA) or 1-800-461-9120 (Canada).

For their help in the preparation of *El Salvador Is My Home*, the editors gratefully thank Professor Michael Fleet, Marquette University, Milwaukee, and Luisa Sandoval.

Library of Congress Cataloging-in-Publication Data

Foran, Eileen.
      El Salvador is my home / adapted from Ronnie Cummins' Children of the world--El Salvador by Eileen Foran ; photographs by Rose Welch.
          p. cm. -- (My home country)
      Includes bibliographical references and index.
      Summary: A look at the life of a twelve-year-old boy and his family who had to move from their farm to a poor section of San Salvador. Includes a section with information on El Salvador.
      ISBN 0-8368-0849-5
      1. El Salvador--Social life and customs--Juvenile literature. [1. Family life--El Salvador. 2. El Salvador.] I. Welch, Rose, ill. II. Cummins, Ronnie. El Salvador. III. Title. IV. Series.
F1483.8.F67   1992
972.8405'3--dc20   92-17724

Edited, designed, and produced by

Gareth Stevens Publishing
1555 North RiverCenter Drive, Suite 201
Milwaukee, Wisconsin 53212, USA

Text, photographs, and format © 1992 by Gareth Stevens, Inc. First published in the United States and Canada in 1992 by Gareth Stevens, Inc. This U.S. edition is abridged from *Children of the World: El Salvador*, © 1990 by Gareth Stevens, Inc., with text by Ronnie Cummins and photographs by Rose Welch.

Series editor: Beth Karpfinger
Cover design: Kristi Ludwig
Designer: Laurie Shock
Map design: Sheri Gibbs

Printed in the United States of America

1 2 3 4 5 6 7 8 9 96 95 94 93 92

My Home Country

EL SALVADOR

IS MY HOME

Adapted from Ronnie Cummins'
Children of the World: El Salvador

by Eileen Foran
Photographs by Rose Welch

Gareth Stevens Publishing
MILWAUKEE

Twelve-year-old Andrés Navarro Aquino comes from a family of nine children. He was born and raised on a farm in rural El Salvador. Until the country's civil war forced them from the farm, the family managed to carve out an existence, raising mainly corn, beans, and chickens. The Navarros now live in a depressed section of San Salvador, working hard once more and looking — along with many other Salvadorans — to their future.

To enhance this book's value in libraries and classrooms, clear and simple reference sections include up-to-date information about El Salvador's geography, demographics, languages, currency, education, culture, industry, and natural resources. *El Salvador Is My Home* also features a large and colorful map, bibliography, glossary, simple index, and research topics and activity projects designed especially for young readers.

The living conditions and experiences of children in El Salvador vary according to economic, environmental, and ethnic circumstances. The reference sections help bring to life for young readers the diversity and richness of the culture and heritage of El Salvador.

My Home Country includes the following titles:

Canada	*Nicaragua*
Costa Rica	*Peru*
Cuba	*Poland*
El Salvador	*South Africa*
Guatemala	*Vietnam*
Ireland	*Zambia*

CONTENTS

LIVING IN EL SALVADOR:
Andrés, a Young Artist

Twelve-year-old Andrés Navarro Aquino lives in El Salvador, Central America's smallest country. Andrés, his parents, and his eight brothers and sisters live in Oscar Romero, a poor neighborhood near San Salvador, the capital of El Salvador. The Navarro family once owned a small farm, but when an air force bomb destroyed it, they had to move to San Salvador.

Andrés stands with his family near Lake Ilopango. His sister Dagoberta (right) stayed at home to guard the house against burglars.

San Salvador rests at the foot of San Salvador Volcano.

Andrés' Home

Andrés remembers when the countryside near his home was attacked by air force helicopters. Soldiers forced the Navarros and their neighbors to move to a refugee camp, where they lived for many years.

When the Navarros moved to San Salvador, they had nowhere to live. They built a simple two-room house. Some of Andrés' neighbors live in shacks made of cardboard, old lumber, and plastic. Andrés feels lucky to live in his sturdy house.

Opposite, top: Oscar Romero is built on land that was once a garbage dump.
Opposite, bottom: The Navarro house is bright blue.

11

Andrés and his best friend, Manuel, talk about their lives before they moved to San Salvador. They talk of the future, too. They worry about being drafted into the army. Andrés thinks that other young men must also be worried, since many have left the country rather than be drafted.

Vendors and children walk along the railroad tracks.

Above: Houses on the hillside seem to be built on top of one another.
Right: Water must be drawn from one of several faucets found near the houses.

Family Life, Past and Present

On their small farm, the Navarros raised corn, beans, and chickens. At harvest time, everyone picked coffee beans on a large plantation. They worked hard, but they enjoyed being together. Andrés misses the farm. Emilio tells him to keep the memories in his heart and the farm will always be with him.

This picture by Andrés shows life as it was on the farm.

Above: Andrés uses his drawings to keep the past alive.
Below: Beans and corn from last year's harvest.

Andrés' youngest brother, Mario, is on his way to the *molina*, or corn grinder.

All the brothers and sisters have chores to do. Francisco and Marcos get water from the pump. Bartholomé carries corn to the grinder. Andrés and Daniel collect firewood. Dagoberta and their mother, Catalina, make breakfast. Mario watches little María. Andrés jokes that Mario might have the hardest job.

Catalina makes tortillas from freshly ground corn.

Daniel sands one of the crosses he has made.

The Crafts and Carpentry Cooperative

After his breakfast, Andrés goes to work at the cooperative. A cooperative, or co-op, is owned by the people who work in it. Andrés and the other young workers are learning how to run a business.

Andrés thinks the co-op is an exciting place to work. Everyone shares equally in the work and in the profits. At co-op meetings, they all vote on how the business should be run.

Top: Andrés designs a cross. Bottom: Bright colors are added to the crosses.

Andrés works in the co-op for four hours in the morning and goes to school for four hours in the afternoon. At the co-op, Andrés creates beautiful items that are sold in North America and Europe.

Andrés also works in the carpentry shop. He makes educational games and puzzles from wood. Schools and day-care centers buy many of these items.

Note cards, paintings, and wooden crosses are some of the things Andrés makes at the co-op.

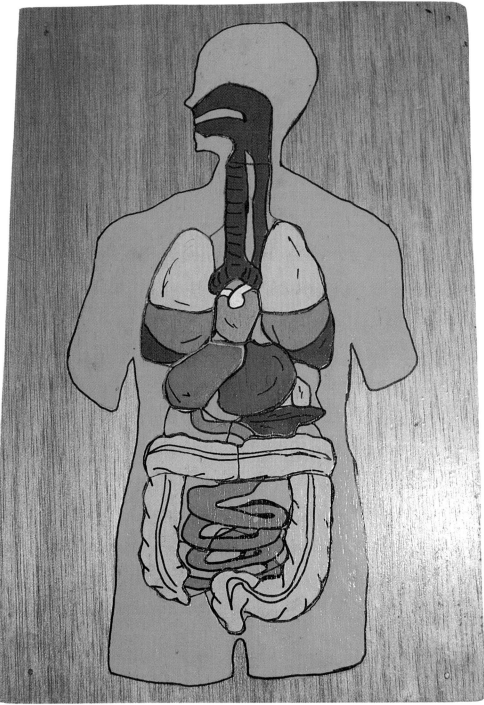

Educational games and puzzles, like this one, sell well at the co-op.

School Life in Oscar Romero

Andrés goes to a Catholic elementary school, where he is in the fourth grade. Reading and social studies are his favorite classes. His least favorite subjects are math, science, and geography.

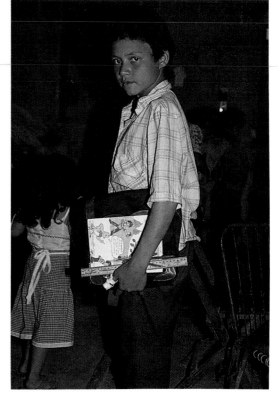

Andrés is ready for school.

At the refugee camp, Andrés did not go to a regular school. He went to a school where there weren't enough teachers to teach all of the students. But Andrés gratefully remembers the volunteer teachers. From them, he learned how to paint and draw.

**Above: Andrés' class photo at the Catholic elementary school in Oscar Romero.
Right: Andrés turns his attention to his studies.**

23

Recess! The fourth-graders release a morning's worth of energy.

Andrés' neighborhood has several church-supported schools. But it has only one public school. Like most Salvadorans, the Navarros can only afford to send the oldest boys to school. Salvadoran girls rarely go to school because they must help with family work.

Top: Andrés' picture shows his class on a field trip.
Bottom: Many churches run their own day-care centers. It may be nap time at this center, but not everyone is sleepy.

Many Salvadoran children have lost one or both parents in the civil war. Andrés thinks being an orphan would be worse than anything he knows of.

Andrés' Favorite Things

After school and on weekends, Andrés finds time for himself. Like many Salvadorans, he loves playing soccer. He and his friends play almost every day.

Andrés also likes to play his guitar. He began three years ago and still plays nearly every day. When he first started, Andrés wondered if he'd ever be good. But his practice has paid off. Now, his family and friends sing along when he plays their favorite songs.

Above: Andrés and his friends play soccer after school.
In a quiet mood, Andrés plays his guitar. ▶

Building a New Neighborhood

Andrés' family has joined a housing cooperative, where people join together to buy land and build houses. Churches often help co-ops get started. They loan families money to build their homes and, in some cases, buy construction materials.

The families in the new community work side by side, forming strong friendships. The work is hard. But soon, they will have new houses and a good neighborhood.

Above (both) and opposite: There's plenty of work to be done before the houses will be complete.

On weekends, the Navarros work at the site of their new house. Andrés' father, Emilio, works there during the week if he cannot find other jobs. When he can, Andrés goes to the site to work beside the older men.

At sunset, Andrés often walks to where the Navarro house will stand. There, looking at the city lit by the beautiful colors of the sunset, Andrés dreams about his new house.

◀ **Andrés works at the site of his family's new home.**
Below: Houses will be built on the hillside.

To the Market

Catalina and Dagoberta do most of the food shopping at the neighborhood market or in San Salvador's central market. The local market is closer, but food is often cheaper downtown.

Andrés likes going to the busy central market in San Salvador. There, he can find everything from food and clothing to school supplies and books.

San Salvador's central market offers more than just food.

32

Andrés Makes a Kite

Andrés, like most children in Oscar Romero, doesn't have much money to spend, so he has learned how to make his own toys and games. Today, he decides to make a kite.

He uses a cornstalk for the frame, a plastic bag for the kite's sail, and a piece of cloth for the tail. Now, Andrés is ready to fly his kite.

Above, top and bottom: Andrés works hard to make a kite that will fly.
Andrés flies the kite from the roof of his house. ▶

Above: Andrés' younger
brothers dance to a
rock 'n' roll tune.
Right: Francisco and
Marcos show off some
of the family's animals.

A Trip to Lake Ilopango

This Sunday, the Navarro family takes the bus to Lake Ilopango. The weather has been hot and sticky for days, so everyone hopes that the lake is nice and cool.

Catalina packs a huge lunch of rice, beans, tortillas, and bananas. After lunch, the children go for a swim. Andrés climbs the bluff. On top, he thinks how nice it would be if his life were as peaceful as this moment.

Andrés, Francisco, Mario, and Marcos enjoy a soda.

Sunday Mass

On Sunday evenings, the family goes to church. Father Pablo reminds everyone that Jesus Christ lived and worked as a carpenter. He encourages people to be proud of their own work.

Above: A North American priest talks to a young parishioner.
After Mass, María gives Mario a quick kiss. ▶

Andrés knows how important the priests are to his community. They work hard so the people of Oscar Romero can have schools, day care centers, and the cooperatives.

A Message of Peace

Andrés draws a greeting card. In English, the card says: "We Salvadorans wish you well. Here, what we like to do is study, work, play ball and marbles, and fly kites. We all go to the playground every day at San Patricio school. My name is Andrés Navarro Aquino. I know many animals: deer, birds, cows, donkeys, dogs, cats. My brothers, sisters, and I send greetings to all children."

Above, top and bottom: Many people gather for a peace march in San Salvador.

No sotros las salvadorenos les deseamas que les baya muy bien en los estados en peramos que se en cuentren bien nosotros aqui lo que los guta es estudiar trabajar los gusta jugar pelota piscucha chivola bamos ala camcha ajugar todos los de la Escuela San Patricio. yo ~~llamo~~
me yamo Andrés Navarro Aquino Conosco muchas animales el venado las aves las vacas burro perro gato y ● mis Hermanitos Saludes atodos los niños san salvador CA

A message of peace from Andrés.

MORE FACTS ABOUT: El Salvador

Official Name: República de El Salvador (ray-POOH-blee-kah deh el SAL-va-dore) Republic of El Salvador

Capital: San Salvador

History

Pipil and Maya Indians were among the original peoples of El Salvador. In 1524, the Spanish invaded, and by 1540, many Indians fled the area. Others died from war, disease, and poverty.

The Spanish soon lost interest in El Salvador, since it was not rich with gold, and by 1821, El Salvador was entirely free of Spanish rule. Throughout the 1800s, five of El Salvador's presidents were overthrown, and two were executed. By 1929, coffee and cotton prices had fallen, and plantation owners could no longer sell their goods. The peasants rebelled. In 1931, General Maximiliano Hernández Martinez took power until 1944, when he was overthrown. A civil war between government and rebel troops has raged in El Salvador since the late 1970s. Until 1984, a military and civilian government led by José Napoleón Duarte controlled El Salvador. In 1989, the Nationalist Republic Alliance party (ARENA) took control of the presidency from Duarte.

Land and Climate

El Salvador, Central America's smallest country, consists of three areas — mountains, the central plateau, and coastal lowlands. The Pacific Ocean lies to its south, Honduras to its northeast, and Guatemala to its northwest. Temperatures range from 73°-80°F (23°-27°C).

People and Language

About 5.5 million people live in El Salvador. Over 90% are *mestizos,* people of mixed Spanish and Indian heritage. Only 2% of the population is full-blooded European. Spanish is the official language. English is studied in many schools.

Education

In El Salvador, the law says that children from age 7 to 12 must attend school. But there are not enough schools in El Salvador, so over 30% of Salvadoran children do not go to school. Students who complete grade school may go on to high school and even to a university. Over 40% of the population can neither read nor write.

Religion

About 85% of El Salvador's population is Roman Catholic. The rest are Protestants or Jews. Many religious groups have taken active roles in the civil rights and political struggles of El Salvador.

Sports and Recreation

Soccer is the national sport of El Salvador. Salvadorans also enjoy basketball, swimming, wrestling, bicycling, and boxing.

The colón is the basic unit of money in El Salvador.

Salvadorans in North America

Between 500,000 and one million Salvadorans have left El Salvador. Many of these people have resettled in other Central American countries, Mexico, the United States, and Canada. Because many refugees have entered North America illegally, government officials do not know the exact number of Salvadorans here.

More Books About El Salvador

El Salvador in Pictures. Lerner Publications
   Dept. of Geography Staff (Lerner)
Enchantment of Central America: El Salvador.
   Carpenter and Baker (Childrens Press)

Glossary of Useful Salvadoran (Spanish) Terms

colón (koh-LONE): the monetary unit of El Salvador.
mestizos (mess-TEE-sohs): people of Indian-Spanish blood.
molino (moh-LEE-noh): a corn-grinding machine
Pipil (PEE-peel): original natives of El Salvador.

Things To Do

1. For a pen pal, write to: Worldwide Pen Friends, P.O. Box 39097, Downey, CA 90241. Be sure to tell them what country you want your pen pal to be from. Also include your full name, age, and address.

2. Andrés lives in a simple house. Compare your home with his. How are they alike? How are they different? Talk with your parents, grand-parents, or someone else whose early homes may not have had modern conveniences.

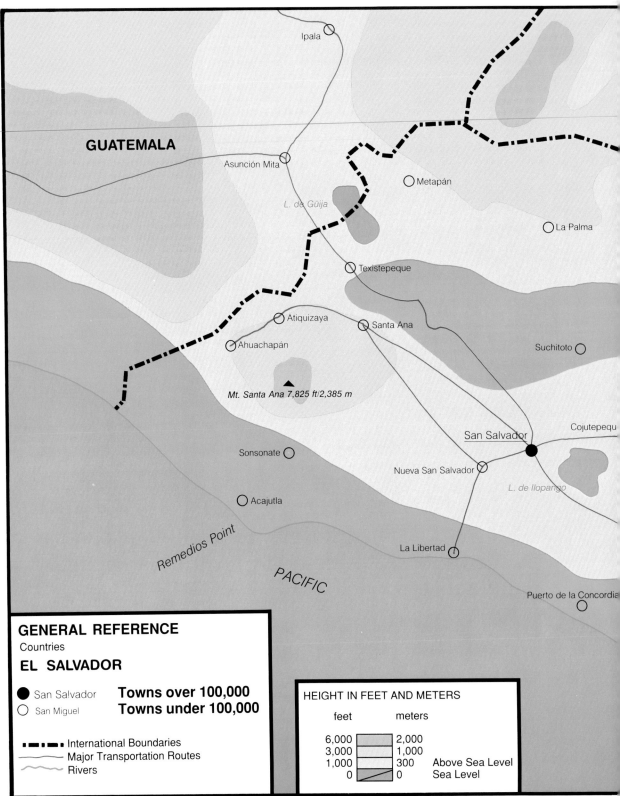

Ipala

GUATEMALA

Asunción Mita

L. de Güija

Metapán

La Palma

Texistepeque

Atiquizaya

Santa Ana

Suchitoto

Ahuachapán

▲
Mt. Santa Ana 7,825 ft/2,385 m

San Salvador

Cojutepequ

Sonsonate

Nueva San Salvador

L. de Ilopango

Acajutla

Remedios Point

La Libertad

PACIFIC

Puerto de la Concordia

GENERAL REFERENCE

Countries

EL SALVADOR

● San Salvador   **Towns over 100,000**
○ San Miguel   **Towns under 100,000**

▪—▪—▪ International Boundaries
—— Major Transportation Routes
〜〜 Rivers

HEIGHT IN FEET AND METERS

feet	meters	
6,000	2,000	
3,000	1,000	
1,000	300	Above Sea Level
0	0	Sea Level

46

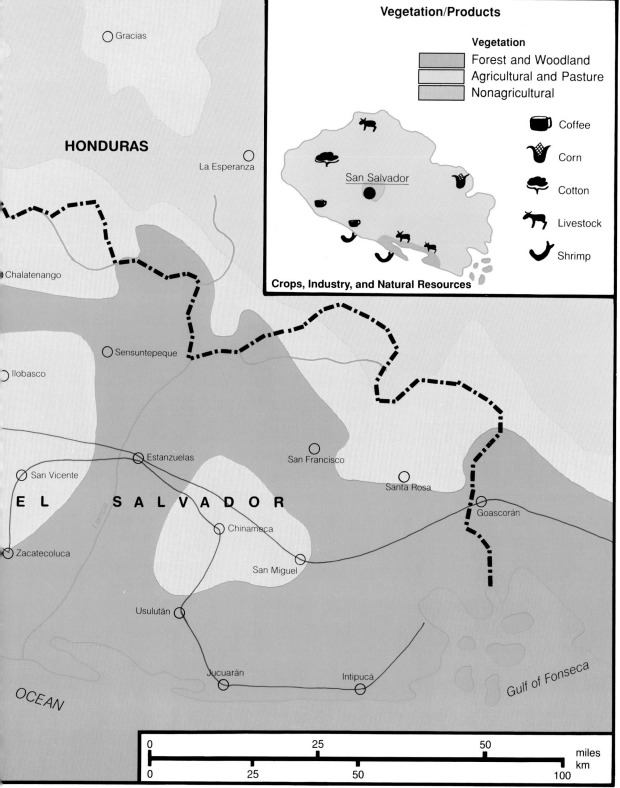

Vegetation/Products

Vegetation
- Forest and Woodland
- Agricultural and Pasture
- Nonagricultural

- Coffee
- Corn
- Cotton
- Livestock
- Shrimp

San Salvador

Crops, Industry, and Natural Resources

Gracias

HONDURAS

La Esperanza

Chalatenango

Sensuntepeque

Ilobasco

Estanzuelas

San Francisco

San Vicente

Santa Rosa

E L   S A L V A D O R

Goascorán

Lempa

Chinameca

Zacatecoluca

San Miguel

Usulután

Jucuarán

Intipucá

OCEAN

Gulf of Fonseca

0		25		50	

miles
km

0	25	50	100

Index